FINALLY AUTISTIC

FINALLY AUTISTIC
Finding my Autism Diagnosis
as a Middle-Aged Female

THERESA WERBA

Bardsinger Books

Books by Theresa Werba

What Was and Is: Formal Poetry and Free Verse
Finally Autistic: Finding My Autism Diagnosis As A Middle-Aged Female
Sonnets
Longer Thoughts
Jesus and Eros: Sonnets, Poems, and Songs
Warning Signs of Abuse: Get Out Early and Stay Free Forever
When Adoption Fails: Abuse, Autism, and the Search for My Identity
Diaper Changes: The Complete Diapering Book and Resource Guide

Copyright © 2024 Theresa Werba All rights reserved.

No part of this book may be reproduced, or stored in a retrieval system, or transmitted in any form or by any means, electronic, mechanical, photocopying, recording, or otherwise, without express written permission of the publisher.

ISBN-13: 978-0-9656955-3-4

Library of Congress Control Number: 2024917838

BARDSINGER BOOKS
www.bardsinger.com
Printed in the United States of America

To Laura, because you saw it first

CONTENTS

PREFACE _____ 9
CHAPTER ONE: GROWING UP AUTISTIC _____ 11
CHAPTER TWO: "A GREAT CHALLENGE": _____ 19
CHAPTER THREE: AUTISM IN ADULTHOOD _____ 43
CHAPTER FOUR: HOW I BECAME DISABLED _____ 59
CHAPTER FIVE: MY AUTISM DIAGNOSIS _____ 77
CHAPTER SIX: SINCE MY DIAGNOSIS _____ 103
CHAPTER SEVEN: ASPERGER'S SPEAKS _____ 113
AFTERWORD _____ 121

PREFACE

Would you believe I was in my mid-50s before I finally figured out what my real problem was? Like many females on the autism spectrum, we are often mis-diagnosed early in life with other neurodivergent conditions, such as ADHD or bipolar disorder. I was diagnosed with bipolar disorder in my 20s but it wasn't until I was 55 that I was finally diagnosed with Level 1 Autism, formerly known as Asperger's Syndrome.

This is the story of my life from the perspective of a little preschool girl who nobody knew how to handle, to a school-age girl who was the smartest, and most talkative, and most disruptive kid in the class, to a blooming teenage singer and writer, to the mental illness of adulthood, and through to my autism diagnosis in middle age.

Finding out I was autistic ended up providing great relief to me, because it explained so many things about my life that made no sense. *Why, with grey hairs abounding, do I still have problems when people ask me, "How are you?" Why did I have the reputation as "Mrs. Blabbermouth" in 5th grade? Why did my adoptive parents abuse me? Why do I still struggle to this day with the give-and-take of everyday conversation?*

I hope my story will be something that resonates with anyone on the autism spectrum, but particularly with older females like myself, who have had a diagnosis later in life, after years of medications and trials and many, many errors. I hope my frank and honest account will be a source of camaraderie and comfort to all who read it.

— Theresa Werba

CHAPTER ONE: GROWING UP AUTISTIC

I was always different from everyone around me. This was partially because I was adopted, and everyone else had genetic parents, and I did not. I was keenly aware of this difference from my earliest age. I always felt I was "on the outside looking in" and wondering why I felt different from everyone around me.

I also was different because I was very smart and I usually responded to the questions in class more quickly and more often than anyone else. I remember my second grade teacher saying "Can someone else besides Theresa answer the question?" I did not feel a sense of superiority but I think this created resentment and jealousy in other students. For my part, I truly enjoyed the learning aspect of school and new knowledge thrilled and delighted me— as it does to this day. But I was utterly oblivious as to how my behavior in class was affecting the other students as well as the teacher—nor did I particularly care at all.

I was also different because I got in trouble and the other students did not. Nobody else was sent to the principal, repeatedly thrown out of the classroom, given bad conduct reports, embarrassed by the teacher, and made to feel horrible about themselves. I felt that no matter what I did or said I was going to get into trouble eventually. At the same time, I did not have any ability to control these behaviors, nor did I understand them in any way, nor were any solutions viable or available to me.

I did have friends growing up and I was okay with 1-1 socialization generally but it was the classroom where I got into trouble. As I see it now, this one success was because I had learned to "mask" very early on, and was able to develop and sustain many close relationships of a 1-1 nature with other children my age because of this learned behavior. It was my "masking" ability that made friendships a possibility to me in childhood, and throughout my life. But I do remember my friend Margot, who was my best friend all though grade school, ceasing to be my friend after we were finally placed in the same classroom in 5th grade. She saw that part of me that was not apparently apparent during 1-1 interaction.

I was lively and talkative and precociously verbal. I was also musically talented and was gifted on the piano as a child. When I got older it was discovered that I had an uncommonly good singing voice and my energies went into vocal music, and writing, for most of my life. I began writing poetry at age ten.

I did have problems as well in my home life. "Home life" consisted of feeling on the outside, not fitting in, wanting to be accepted but being rejected, trying to be understood, not understanding what I was doing wrong, always striving to be loved, wanting to communicate but missing the mark, feeling that no matter what I did or didn't do it wasn't enough. I discuss my life as an adoptee in my book *When Adoption Fails: Abuse, Autism, and the Search for My Identity*.

In the book I mention the fact that in my adoptive parents' defense, they did not know what they were dealing with, and were helpless and clueless as to how to help me. Autism was not mainstream in the 1960s and 1970s and certainly not on the radar for girls. Autism in girls is just now coming around to be understood and accepted as a thing but in my childhood it was unheard of. I do not remember ever being evaluated by a psychologist or psychiatrist for anything. I was left to flounder on my own, trying to deal with the world as best as I could, trying not to upset everyone with my just being there, or worse yet, opening my mouth.

My adoptive mother would say to me, "Theresa, when you are talking, you need to stop and let the other person say something, so they can have a turn." I am really glad she said this to me. I did apply this principle throughout my life, without knowing why I had to. To this day, I have to think very hard about when to turn the conversation back on to the other person, and I usually vie in favor of turning it to the other person if I have any doubts, because it's better to be safe than sorry. But left to my own devices, I could literally talk an hour straight or more, and have more to say. I have the capacity to have a long, one-sided conversation with myself. But at least my adoptive mother was trying to help me in this case, and in this case that bit of advice has really helped me regulate my verbal discourse throughout my life.

Somehow I did learn eventually to "mask" and this worked extremely well in the context of my eventually becoming a performer. When I am on stage it is perfect: I am the one delivering, the audience is listening, and it is *not* a two-way communication. I could do an hour-long performance, and then just leave. I never understood why this ended up being a better occupation for me than a regular job, but I had never done well with regular jobs, so gigs and performances worked really well for me. I truly am happiest when I am in front of an audience performing— which these days is not singing but performing my poetry.

I did learn early on to "put on my face" as I used to call it, without even knowing it was a thing that autistic people do. I just figured out a way to get along with people, and this involved a bit of pretend. That is not the real me they are seeing. If they saw the real me they would get tired and bored, because I would go on and on about something that interests me. But I learned somewhere along the line that you can do this pretending, and people become your friend (and eventually boyfriend) because you likeable. So I became likeable to some degree, because of my masking. This led to many close friendships throughout my life, as well as more lovers and entanglements than I care to remember.

As a child, I remember rocking my head back and forth, from side to side, at night in bed. I realize now that this was a kind of self-soothing behavior among autistic people known as stimming. I also used to hide under tables and lock myself in closets. I liked small spaces like carboard boxes made into playhouses. I would make nests in them with blankets and pillows. This was very soothing and comforting to me.

My behavioral problems in school were legion. I was repeatedly thrown out of the 2nd grade classroom and made to sit across the hall in the third grade classroom. My teacher once got mad that I twirled around to show my skirt twirling, and she threw me into the 3rd grade classroom. I remember her saying, as she brought me to those older kids in the room across the hall, saying, "Are you allowed to twirl your dress in a classroom?" It was so embarrassing and uncomfortable to be put in the 3rd grade classroom. The kids were so much bigger than I was, and they would stare at me, wondering no doubt what I did to deserve to be there.

When I was at the end of 4th grade I had a car accident because I stupidly ran across the street into an oncoming car. I was in the hospital for a period of time, and my classmates wrote a poem for me. I remember a line which said "Although you chitter-chatter, it really doesn't matter, because we love you, and are crying 'Boo-hoo.'" I really do try to imagine myself as the little girl who couldn't stop talking in class.

In 5th grade my teacher called me "Mrs. Blabbermouth" and taped my mouth with masking tape and stuck me in the back of the class. I remember feeling really embarrassed, keeping my teary eyes down, hoping that somehow this situation would just go away. *Why do I keep getting into trouble?*

When I got to adolescence, I began cutting my ankles and my hands. I would throw plates and bang my head against the wall. I believe I got into states of irrationality, because things were not the way I thought they were supposed to be, or I was frustrated over a situation which wasn't what I expected it to be. I also remember saying "People stab themselves to let the pain out." I really was hurting and I was in pain. But I never understood the reason why I did the things I did.

I kept lists of all my boyfriends and my friends. I did this many times over the years. I'd categorize them and re-categorize them and put them in columns in chronological order. I also made lists of all the books I had read. This activity was very soothing and comforting to me.

I used to also come home from school and do math problems. I really enjoyed going over them again and again. It was delightful to me to find a solution that was repeatable and dependable and was fun to figure out.

The subways were always too loud for me. I was literally the only person standing on the platform with my fingers in my ears. I am not sure why the concept of ear plugs never occurred to me but I did have (and still do have) sensitivity to loud noises. I never liked loud rock concerts or even loud symphonic music, though I was trained as a classical musician.

I was never good in sports. They would always pick me last for baseball and other team games. I did, however, learn to swim competently and I swim to this day. But I cannot play sports, or even understand sports, or why sports would be interesting to anyone. My fine motor skills, such as are used for sewing or piano playing, are well-developed, but my gross motor skills have always been lacking. I bump into things. I bump into people. When I was a kid I used to trip and fall a lot. I considered myself awkward and uncoordinated. Dancing is also an issue— I feel very self-conscious when I have to dance because I know how doofy and spastic I look. My body image has been tainted by my inability to move gracefully or smoothly though places and among people.

 I somehow remained a happy and optimistic child even though I had so many behavioral problems at school and difficulties at home. I always looked forward to each day with anticipation and expectation. I loved learning (as I still do) and I loved doing creative projects like making Indian bead bracelets, paper mâché figurines, and learning to sew. I loved doing my schoolwork and I loved playing and practicing the piano. I began to write songs in 4th grade and I delighted in my musical ability. I sang my first solo in 6th grade and this went on to my acquiring two degrees in vocal music performance. I loved riding my bike alone when we were at our county house, and I would pedal miles and miles around unhindered and alone.

 Even though my relationship with my adoptive parents was dysfunctional and abusive, I still loved them and continued to approach each day with hope and positivity. Eventually I did not love my adoptive father anymore though I loved my adoptive mother till the day she died and beyond.

I began to write poetry when I was about ten. I remember something I wrote about the water lapping against the shore, "like a mother's gentle kiss to her babe." I went on to get published in the high school journal, and then many publications throughout my adult life.

I remember the junior high I eventually attended was throwing out a bunch of books. I remember gathering some and reading them. I was still in grade school but I was reading these junior high English textbooks. I enjoyed this activity immensely. I also would often read the dictionary for fun and I have always taken great pleasure in looking up words for their precise meaning, etymology, and usage.

I loved my solitude because it was during these times of being alone with myself that I could learn, and create, and enjoy life completely.

Childhood was difficult, challenging, painful, and even sad for me, but I maintained a sanguine optimism, an eagerness for the joys and discoveries of life, and a hopefulness for a happy, fulfilling future.

And as I grew into an adolescent and then an adult, I continued to be beset by behavioral problems. The roots and seeds of my lifetime challenges and issues are elucidated in the following school records from preschool, grade school, and junior high school.

CHAPTER TWO: "A GREAT CHALLENGE"
MY SCHOOL RECORDS

I always knew something was wrong with me because I was always getting into trouble. I had behavioral problems since preschool which continued through grade school and into junior high school which the following records will elucidate. Once I got into high school these issues seemed to have dissipated somewhat but throughout my adulthood I had exhibited aberrant behaviors which have plagued me all my life. I never understood why these things were happening or why I behaved the way I did. I did not understand why certain things would affect me to the point of irrational outbursts or bizarre behavior or why I had such a hard time in most public situations.

One thing about autism is that you do not develop it, and you do not grow out of it. You are born with it and you have it your entire life. I wanted to start with my records because they are immutable evidence of something terribly amiss with me from a very young age.

As a bit of background, you should know that I was adopted. The story of my adoption is covered in my book *When Adoption Fails: Abuse, Autism, and the Search for My Identity* but I present some information here as a bit of background.

I was born in July of 1962 to a 16-year old sex worker who tried to raise me for 2 ½ months and then gave me away into the foster care system. I was then taken care of by a foster mother with two young boys who wanted to adopt me. She had me from the age of 2 ½ months to 13 months. The adoption was not permitted to proceed so I wound up getting adopted by an older, childless couple who had roots in a religious New-Age type of cult. I remained with this couple until I was fifteen. I had a dysfunctional relationship with my adoptive parents that included emotional and physical abuse by my adoptive parents and sexual assault by my adoptive brother.

I wrote an autobiography when I was in second grade and I said that I was "a baby that cried a lot." This information came from my adoptive mother. But imagine that I had three mothers by the time I was thirteen months old. Anyone would cry a lot over that. But were there other reasons?

When I got into preschool, it was clear that I was different and that I had behavioral problems. I am fortunate enough to have detailed reports from my preschool years which describe and illustrate my behavioral difficulties that were already manifest at this age. There are three separate reports here.

DEVELOPMENTAL REPORT

February 15, 1966
#1 Four Year old Group
Report by Virginia Cramer

THERESA ARLUCK

Age: 3 years, 7 months

PHYSICAL DEVELOPMENT

Theresa is a small girl with blonde curly hair, large blue eyes, and a very pretty face. She is a very active child is developing large-muscle abilities as can be seen in her increased proficiency at running, climbing, pulling, and swinging. She has learned to ride a tricycle since beginning school. Theresa is right-handed and has good small-muscle facilities— she enjoys manipulative materials such as pegs and boards, puzzles and small plastic building blocks and works nicely with these. Theresa has missed several days for colds but it no more than average for this age.

INTELLECTUAL DEVELOPMENT

Theresa has a good vocabulary, pronounces her words well and speaks well-formed and complete sentences. She shows good reasoning abilities concerning the home and school environments. She remembers our class experiences and discussions and will remarks on these things to the teachers. Theresa is capable of good concentration, particularly with the expressive materials, but generally needs encouragement to stay with the blocks and manipulative materials. She responds to this encouragement and completes her task, this gaining a sense of achievement and mastery. Theresa's art work shows good imagination and her collage work is well-balanced and organized with both colors and forms. Theresa has a friendly sense of humor and laughs or smiles readily at fun-making. She has a good visual perception but often needs aural focus— she does not always listen when it would help her to do so and needs to be directed to "listen with your ears." Once focused, she responds readily, indicating good understanding of verbal directions and requests.

EMOTIONAL SOCIAL DEVELOPMENT

From her beginning of her late entrance into the group, Theresa has been trusting and affectionate with her teachers. It is not always easy for her to cooperate with school routines but this varies from day to day. The teachers have to be certain of Theresa's attention as she often concentrates intensely elsewhere and does not hear directions or reminders.

Theresa has made a very significant adjustment to the group. She showed signs of little social experience prior to school and had developed no techniques for relating to her peers. She tended to dive for things she wanted, whether another child was or was not using them, and would cry if she could not have what she wanted immediately. This still occurs with the materials and especially favors but with many things she can ask and await her turn. It is suggested that Theresa *have some home visits at her home for lunch and a short play period with some of the children (one at a time) with whom she relates well. Experiences such as these in addition to her school experiences with a group will offer her added opportunities to develop relationships. Although most of her play is alone or parallel, many of the children accepted Theresa into the group very quickly and would ask about her when she was absent. She is always sympathetic when a child is bumped or upset, coming close to them, patting them gently, and asking, "What's the matter, honey?"*

Theresa is independent about toileting, washing, and manages her orthopedic shoes surprisingly well. It is still difficult for her to remain at the table during juice and to relax during rest time. She is unable to help very much with clean-up and needs specific guidance regarding each piece she has used and could put away.

WORK AND PLAY PREFERENCES AND ABILITIES

Theresa has responded to all areas of the curriculum at some time since the beginning of her school experience. She is especially interested in the art materials and works intensively with her hands in clay, dough, finger and brush paint, collage, chalk and paper construction. Theresa tends more and more to stay with these tasks and completes them. She loves the housekeeping area and cooks and serves with much zest. She likes to dress up in ladies' dresses and in men's clothing.

The listening times are hardest for Theresa but her natural musical ability and love for stories help her with self-control and she is showing growth here.

<u>Remarks</u>

Theresa has developed in many ways since starting school and we are finding her a rewarding child to work with at Jack and Jill School.

June, 1966

Dear Dr. and Mrs. Arluck,

Theresa seems to have had a generally more happy time in school during this latter part of the school year. She played most enjoyably with Danny, Michele, Jean, and Avie in many kinds of dramatic play which, along with the expressive materials, is Theresa's favorite and most accomplished area of activity.

It continued to be difficult to communicate to Theresa the need for group behavior. She ran away from the group many times or hurried into places where children were asked *not to go, wide-eyed with delight, seeming to lack any awareness of breaking with group requirements. The problem of sharing shifted from small individually-employed objects to large group-employed objects, such as the rocking board in the yard. This piece of equipment accommodates four to six children at a time. Often Theresa would get on and cry and scream when the other children would not get off or would approach for a turn. She was indistractable and inconsolable at these times and the teachers had to let her cry these difficulties out. Perhaps some firm limits, consistently established and required at home this summer, may aid Theresa towards following group disciplines at school next year.*

Theresa became very interested in stories and was generally an attentive listener. Her attention span has increased steadily during the year and she completed most of the tasks she began on a good-to-high working level. Her verbal pattern and vocabulary continued to develop and become richer.

We have had an interesting year with Theresa. We wish all of you a most happy summer.

Sincerely yours,
Virginia Cramer
Group Teacher

DEVELOPMENTAL REPORT

Name: Theresa Arluck
Date February 1967
Teacher: Margaret Wright

<u>Physical Development:</u>

Theresa is a little girl with a slender body and an intelligent face with very expressive eyes. She is an active child who has a drive to keep moving and often does not look where she is going. She often stumbles and falls. When she climbs and rides a tricycle, her large muscle coordination is good. Theresa's small muscles are very well developed and she can assemble pieces quickly when working puzzles, use laces to follow patterns on sewing cards and manipulate scissors with ease when cutting. Theresa missed some time from school because of colds but she has a good average attendance.

<u>Intellectual Development:</u>

Theresa is an intelligent child. She has a large vocabulary with a good understanding of the words she uses. She is able to express herself quite well at discussion time giving interesting and intelligent answers to questions relating *to the subject we are talking about. At story time she often talks and disturbs other children who want to listen. When she does settle down she has the power to concentrate.*

During the work-play period at the beginning of the school year, Theresa kept going at a frantic pace from one activity to another. She showed curiosity in experimenting in all areas of the program but her interest span was very short. It seemed she was torn with a desire to do many things at once. The teachers have tried to help her slow down and to think about the choice of activity and then spend enough time with it to have a feeling of accomplishment. This was a slow process but now she is spending longer periods of time when she uses the art and craft materials and her finished products are showing thoughtfulness and are often creative. Now Theresa is beginning to have more satisfying play in the housekeeping and block building areas because she is learning the necessity of give and take. She knows now she cannot always have the toy she wants and that in school it is necessary to take turns. This has seemed most difficult for Theresa to understand. It has been the cause of a great deal of crying and even though we think that Theresa is learning she needs constant reminders. We believe that when Theresa has better emotional control she will be a happier child, therefore we spend a great deal of time trying to make consistent explanation and appeals for her cooperation in overcoming this immature behavior.

Social-Emotional Development: Relationships to Adults in School:

Theresa is friendly and outgoing with her teachers. She is a verbal child and enjoys talking to the teachers and have them listen to her. Because of her problem of sharing and taking turns there are many emotional outbursts and lots of crying. However Theresa never holds any resentment. Instead she comes to us for help in solving her problems and is often quite affectionate.

Behavior in School Routine:

Theresa is able to take care of her personal needs at school. She helps in removing and putting on her outside clothing, when we go and come from the play-yard. She enjoys juice and cookie time. Theresa is able to relax and be quiet at rest time.

Work and Play Preferences and Abilities:

Theresa likes to use all the art and craft materials. She spends longer periods now working on special projects with a teacher and a group of children doing something together. She has used all the forms of paint introduced in our program. She *has played with dough and recently modeled with clay. She likes to participate in water play.*

Theresa has spent time in the housekeeping area doing things with other children to dramatize the adult world as she sees it. She also sometimes chooses to go to the block corner and build with two or three children working together.

Theresa has used all the toys and equipment on the open shelves for the children's selection. She is especially quick to work each new puzzle and game that appears on the shelf.

<u>Remarks:</u>

Theresa is an interesting and intelligent child. She has offered her teachers a great challenge. We think she needs constant reminders to follow simple rules and regulations. This is needed in order that she develop her full potential.

When giving these report a cursory glance, it seems that I had ADHD symptoms as much as what could be identified as autism symptoms: *"needs aural focus— she does not always listen when it would help her to do so"*; *"she often concentrates intensely elsewhere"*; *"an active child who has a drive to keep moving"*; *"kept going at a frantic pace from one activity to another"*; *" her interest span was very short. It seemed she was torn with a desire to do many things at once."*

But then there are the many indicators that I have problems with socialization and emotional control, signs of autism in a young child: *"It is not always easy for her to cooperate with school routines"*; *"She tended to dive for things she wanted, whether another child was or was not using them, and would cry if she could not have what she wanted immediately"*; *"It continued to be difficult to communicate to Theresa the need for group behavior"*; *"seeming to lack any awareness of breaking with group requirements"*; *"when Theresa has better emotional control she will be a happier child"*; *"many emotional outbursts and lots of crying"*; *"enjoys talking to the teachers and have them listen to her"*; *"constant reminders to follow simple rules and regulations."*

I am also fortunate to have most of my grade school report cards. Following are five years of report cards from 2nd through 6th grade. As you can see, when I got to grade school I was predominantly cited as having issues with self-control.

Theresa Arluck
Class 2-214
Teacher: Mrs. Sorkin

MARKING PERIODS

All ratings (E= excellent, G= good, F=fair, U=unsatisfactory) were good or excellent in all marking three periods, except:

ORAL LANGUAGE

Listens carefully: U, U-F, U

All ratings (S= satisfactory, I=improving, U=unsatisfactory) were S in all three marking periods except:

PERSONAL and SOCIAL DEVELOPMENT
Shows respect: U, U, S
Carries out responsibilities: I-U, I-U, S
Obeys rules and regulations: U, U, U
Shows self-control: U, U, U

<u>Teacher Comments</u>

Theresa is a very lively child. She is alert and interested in practically everything that is going on. Although her level of work is quite good for her age, I think she can do even better. She is reluctant to stop once activity and begin another and frequently has difficulty with directions as a result. She also resents not being called on ALL the time. There is a <u>very</u> intelligent and capable child. Her lack of self-control often makes it difficult for her and those around her. Her very strong bid for attention needs working with both in and out of school. I think it is important that we discuss this.

REPORT TO PARENTS

Sept 1970-June 1971
Theresa Arluck

Class 3-216
Teacher: Mrs. P. Herman

MARKING PERIODS

All ratings (E= excellent, G= good, F=fair, U=unsatisfactory) were good or excellent in all marking three periods, except:

ORAL LANGUAGE
Listens carefully: G, F-F, F

All ratings (S= satisfactory, I=improving, U=unsatisfactory) were S in all three marking periods except:

PERSONAL and SOCIAL DEVELOPMENT

Obeys rules and regulations: I, S-I, S-I
Shows self-control: I, I, I

<u>Teacher Comments</u>

Period 1: Theresa is aware of her need to improve in the areas indicated, and makes a real effort to do so. With our help, I'm sure she'll show she can.

Period 2: Theresa still forgets, despite her election and her recent responsibility as vice-president, that she must develop more self-control. Let's keep working on that. Other areas show improvement.

Period 3: There is still the need for allowing others to speak and to think of the rights of the group. On the positive side, Theresa has made many contributions, especially in creative ideas, dramatics, music.

REPORT TO PARENTS

Sept 1971-June 1972

Theresa Arluck
Class 4-308
Mrs. Bronn

MARKING PERIODS

All ratings (E= excellent, G= good, F=fair, U=unsatisfactory) were good or excellent in all marking three periods, except:

ORAL LANGUAGE
Listens carefully: G, G, E

All ratings (S= satisfactory, I=improving, U=unsatisfactory) were S in all three marking periods except:

PERSONAL and SOCIAL DEVELOPMENT
Shows respect: U, E, E
Obeys rules and regulations: U, I, S-I
Shows self-control: U, I, S-I

<u>Teacher Comments</u>

Period 1: Theresa must work on achieving greater self-control as she finds it difficult to discipline her desire to call out or interrupt while others are speaking. We are working on this.
Period 2: Theresa has shown great improvement in controlling her behavior. However she must remember that others be given a chance to speak and learn to wait her turn.
Period 3: I'll certainly miss Theresa's exciting personality.

REPORT TO PARENTS

Sept 1972-June 1973
Theresa Arluck
Class 5-400
Mrs. Rubenstein

MARKING PERIODS

All ratings (E= excellent, G= good, F=fair, U=unsatisfactory) were good or excellent in all marking three periods, except:

ORAL LANGUAGE
Listens carefully: F, G-F,G-F

All ratings (S= satisfactory, I=improving, U=unsatisfactory) were S in all three marking periods except:

PERSONAL and SOCIAL DEVELOPMENT
Shows respect: I, S, S
Obeys rules and regulations: S-I, S-I, S-I
Shows self-control: I, I, I

<u>Teacher Comments</u>

Period 1: Theresa is very capable and does very good work. She needs to develop greater self-control and be aware of other people's rights. I would like to discuss this with you.

Period 2: Theresa continues to do very good work. She still has a problem with self-control but she is working on it.

Period 3: Theresa has been trying very hard to exercise more self-control but has a long way to go to this end. She seems to be more able to understand how this irritates her peers.

REPORT TO PARENTS

Sept 1973-1974
Theresa Arluck
6-403
Mr. Genkins

MARKING PERIODS

All ratings (E= excellent, G= good, F=fair, U=unsatisfactory) were good or excellent in all marking three periods, except:

ORAL LANGUAGE
Listens carefully: F, F-F-U

All ratings (S= satisfactory, I=improving, U=unsatisfactory) were S in all three marking periods except:

PERSONAL and SOCIAL DEVELOPMENT
Shows respect: S, S, U
Carries out responsibilities: S, S, I
Obeys rules and regulations: S, S, I
Shows self-control: I-U, I, U

WORK HABITS
Follows directions S, S, U

Completes work on time S, S, U

<u>Teacher Comments</u>

Period 1: Theresa is a bright pupil who does well in class. Sometimes there is a problem with self-control.
Period 2: There is still a problem with self-control. However, I did notice Theresa working very effectively with young children.
Period 3: Theresa is very talented but she has not gotten control of herself. I would say that all efforts should be made to conquer these problems.

Throughout grade school I had consistently unsatisfactory ratings in listening, following directions and showing self-control. *"She is reluctant to stop once activity and begin another and frequently has difficulty with directions as a result. She also resents not being called on ALL the time... her lack of self-control often makes it difficult for her and those around her;" "There is still the need for allowing others to speak and to think of the rights of the group"; " Theresa must work on achieving greater self-control as she finds it difficult to discipline her desire to call out or interrupt while others are speaking...she must remember that others be given a chance to speak and learn to wait her turn"; "She needs to develop greater self-control and be aware of other people's rights... Theresa has been trying very hard to exercise more self-control but has a long way to go to this* end. She seems to be more able to understand how this irritates her peers"; "Theresa is very talented but she has not gotten control of herself."

When I got to junior high school I began to sing in earnest. I realize now why singing really worked for me as an autistic person. I was able to do a kind of one-sided communication with people who were there to listen to me. Ideal!! I had control of the situation and it was all about me and what mattered to me. And there wasn't any give-and-take, something I have struggled in vain to master all my life. Whatever natural musical talents I had really found their home inside my autistic sensibilities. While I was getting solos and leads in the vocal program, I still struggled with the issues of self-control. I am fortunate to have my report cards from all three years of junior high.

REPORT TO PARENTS

7-9 (7th) Sept 1974- June 1975
Theresa Arluck Mr. Anstadt

Personal Adjustment *(S=satisfactory; N= needs improvement; NI= not improved) for 3 marking periods:*

Courtesy: N,N, N, S
Effort: N, S, S, S

Responsibility: N,S, S, S
Self-Control: N,N,N, S

First Report— Greater effort needed in social studies and math; also improvement needed in some conduct grades.

Second Report— Show some improvement but still more needed in social studies.

Third Report— Much improvement in conduct.

4th Report— improvement made in most subjects.

REPORT TO PARENTS

Sept 1975-June 1976
8-1 (8th)
Theresa Arluck
Mrs. Waller

Personal Adjustment *(S=satisfactory; N= needs improvement; NI= not improved) for 3 marking periods:*

Courtesy: S- N,S, S, S
Effort: S-N, S, N, S

Responsibility: S,S, S, S
Self-Control: N,N,N, S

First Report— Good grades Theresa <u>but</u> you must improve your homeroom behavior.

Second Report— Nice grades <u>but</u> you must improve your behavior in classes as well as homeroom.

Third report— This would be a nice report card except for your gym failure and your homeroom conduct— too talkative.

REPORT TO PARENTS

Sept 1976- June 1977
Class 9-1 (9th grade)
Theresa Arluck
Mr. Harman H. Shell

Personal Adjustment *(S=satisfactory; N= needs improvement; NI= not improved) for 3 marking periods:*

Courtesy: S, N, S, S
Effort: S, S, S, S
Responsibility: S,S, S, S

Self-Control: S,N,N, N

First Report— Theresa has done well this period.

Second Report— Theresa needs more self-control.

Third Report— Theresa has shown some improvement.

Fourth Report— Theresa has made some improvement this year.

And even into junior high school the reports say much the same as they always did: *"improvement needed in some conduct grades"; "you must improve your homeroom behavior"; "you must improve your behavior in classes as well as homeroom"; "your homeroom conduct— too talkative"; "Theresa needs more self-control."*

Things did get better for me as I developed the ability to "mask"—the face I learned to put on when singing and in social activity. I think I got away with a lot of my behavior as I got older because artistic people are often kind of eccentric to begin with. I basically fit in with the quirky musician and writer types. The masking worked especially well for me with 1-1 interaction and I have been able to have close relationships throughout the years because of this learned behavior. It definitely does not come naturally to me.

This chapter provides the background I wanted to share about my childhood as an autistic girl, in an age when autism was not as well-understood as it is today, especially in girls. But the evidence of my place on the autism spectrum is clear to anyone who examines my history now. I am so thankful that I somehow preserved these records all these years. When I read them before my autism diagnosis, I was trying to fit all of it into the frame of reference as an individual with bipolar disorder. But it never made any sense to me. I knew something was definitely wrong, or different, with me, but it did not seem to make sense in terms of only mood swings. I now know that I was always wired differently, that my neurodivergent brain operated differently from others around me, and that I had challenges throughout my life that were the result of my autism and nothing else.

CHAPTER THREE: AUTISM IN ADULTHOOD

Now that I have my diagnosis it is reassuring to me that I wasn't insane, or even bi-polar, but an autism level 1 female struggling throughout life with a condition she did not know she had, let alone understood.

The following are some anecdotes from my adulthood that I remember that stand out in terms of their peculiarity and specificity to my autism. They are painfully embarrassing but in looking back I can see that it was not my fault and I did not know how to manage my behavior or my reactions to the world around me.

I was still a teenager when I abandoned my singing career to go into nursing. I was heavily influenced by my boyfriend at the time but I also felt it was some kind of calling. I had recently converted to Christianity and was full of religious zeal and fervor. I enrolled in an LPN program at the local community college.

At some point there was a psych rotation and we were required to interact with psychiatric patients. I remember talking to this guy and I was trying to be helpful so I started "witnessing" to him and telling him about Jesus. (This is something that is encouraged as part of demonstrating one's faith in the Christian circles I was part of). Somehow my instructor got wind of it and I was thrown out of the program. She also made some comment about how I wiped my nose on the sleeve of my shirt but mainly I was dismissed for violating the rules, rules I didn't even know existed.

In my early 20s I got a job doing activities in a nursing home. I remember not liking my boss or the social worker. It built up to a great deal of tension and discomfort. It boiled over when I forfeited my job one day by saying *"Dale is a bitch and Mrs. Kraus is a witch!"* I quit the job and did not understand what caused me to have an adult version of a meltdown.

When I was in my mid-20s I was in a singing group performing at the Citicorp building. We had a rehearsal and then we had a break. I meandered over to this Mexican restaurant and proceeded to read the overhead menu. I ordered something. I am not sure what happened next exactly but they told me what I wanted was not on the menu. *But it says it's available!* I got so angry that I pushed the cash register onto the floor and walked out. I realized that I could get arrested for what I just did, so I walked around the block and did a kind of detour before getting back into the Citicorp building and performing in the concert like nothing ever happened.

Around the same time in life (mid-20s) I worked for an agent of musical acts. For some time I was designing pamphlets and other advertising materials. I had a weird relationship with the boss— he seemed to like my work but overall I know I was getting on his nerves. I am not sure what happened but he got really exasperated at me one day, threw his scissors on the floor, and told me I was fired.

Also around the same time in life I remember working for a nursing home in the activities department. I was told by the supervisor that I was not dressing professionally. I used to wear long skirts! Not sure why this was such a big deal but somehow I was missing some clues about social propriety.

At this time I became utterly obsessed with my ex-fiancée. I got so obsessed with him that I managed to sneak into his apartment when he was gone one day and I hid in the bathroom closet until he came back. I waited for hours in there. I scared the crap out of him by standing at the foot of his bed once he was asleep and woke him up. I became entirely focused and one-minded about this man and was so for many years.

Into my 30s I had a job answering phones and taking orders for my friend's home business. I was told repeatedly that I sounded "rude" and that I needed to be nicer to the customers on the phone. But I have always been called rude on the phone, as well as often shouting and yelling and cursing at the person on the other end. I still struggle with this issue to this day. I have also been accused of being rude (many times over) during most social interactions of a superficial nature.

I had an incident at the DMV where I planned to renew my license and I was told I could not bring my infant daughter into the testing area. I got very irate. *But I planned on having her with me! You cannot change the plan!! This is not what I expected!!!* But I got so angry with them and acting so inappropriately that I was thrown out of the building.

I had an incident in my 30s where I took a situation quite literally and it cost me my inheritance. This is described in more detail in my book *When Adoption Fails: Autism, Abuse, and the Search for My Identity*. My adoptive mother's dog bit one of my little daughters in the face. I thought very literally of the situation: dog bite=animal control. I told my adoptive mother that my daughter was bit and that I needed to call animal control. She responded "If you call animal control I will disinherit you and you will get nothing from me." In that moment I could not think beyond the literal nature of the situation. *Could I have not called? Could I have tried to reason with my adoptive mother? Could I have realized that this basically would end up ruining my financial future for the rest of my life? Was my daughter really in danger? Was I thinking rationally? Was I being too literal and not seeing the situation in a more nuanced way?*

I called animal control and then we left my mother's home and nine months later she was dead and I was disinherited.

In my 40s I had trouble with a choir that I was part of. I continually had issues with the choir director and at one point impulsively quit the choir. I became hopelessly irrational. I literally quit and walked out the door during the rehearsal.

I also had issues with a homeschool choir that I was conducting. I remember the final concert. I had told the students that they needed to be there for the warm-ups or they would not be able to sing. Of course a family with two kids showed up late. I refused to let the children sing but did let them stand with the choir. I was rigid and inflexible about this. This angered the parent very much and she complained to the director of our homeschool co-op. I was asked not to come back the following year.

One of the bigger issues was regarding Santa Claus. I was substitute teaching in a Kindergarten class. One of the assignments was to read *The Night Before Christmas* to the children. I was very much against this as I did not believe that teaching children a lie or a fairy tale as truth is ever a good thing. I never taught my kids to believe in Santa Claus but to believe that I and their father gave them their Christmas presents. This was definitely part of my firmly-held religious and moral beliefs. I was rigid and inflexible when confronted with this dilemma and I could not see any nuanced resolution to my problem. What I could have done was go to the principal and simply explained that reading a story about Santa Claus to the children violated my religious beliefs and that I wanted to be excused from reading it. The other thing I could have done was to not have read it at all— would anyone have ever known?

But I chose to read the story to them, with some modification. I told the children that Santa Claus was actually a man named Nicholas, sometimes called Saint Nicholas or Saint Nick, who went around giving gifts to the poor and sick died in the 4th century. I think I went as far as to say that St Nick is not alive anymore. Of course then one of the children went to their mother and said "Teacher said Santa Claus is dead." I ended up having to go to the principal's office and explain myself.

Somehow it wound up in the local news and then I was asked to do an interview where I explained my actions. I ended up getting hate mail from all over the country. Of course I was taken off the substitute teaching list for that school. I really became public enemy #1 over this one school assignment!

I also had great difficulty when I was a lecturer in music at a public university. This was a part-time adjunct position that I took when I graduated my master's degree program. The biggest problem for me was unexpected behavior by the students. It was hard enough standing in front of forty kids and trying to teach them something about Western music or music fundamentals, but when they did something I did not anticipate it made me freeze up, then get very angry, like a kind of mini-meltdown that I tried desperately to control. Things happened that I couldn't anticipate, and I was not in control of the situation, as I would be when performing in front of a crowd. It was one of the hardest things I ever did. What did help was my "masking" persona of the performer— I could put it on and it was not me and somehow I could get through it. Most of my student reviews at the time said I was too strict and graded too severely. After a few semesters I was not asked back to teach Western music or music fundamentals, but I was kept on to conduct the campus choir, which for some reason was a success. My rating on Rate My Professor was a 1.8 when most faculty have ratings in the 3-5s.

The one saving grace for me was my talent for singing, and now performing my poetry. It was through this medium that

I figured out how to "mask"—how to act publicly in a way that was social acceptable—as I could stand on a stage and sing or recite, and there was separation between me and the crowd, but I could still communicate with them through the music, or my words. I learned how to "put on my face," as I used to call it, before going into a performance, and now a reading. I always had difficulty looking at the audience in the eyes so I would look over their heads when I sang. I do this when I recite my poetry today. Often you would find me singing with my eyes closed. But in this scenario I am in total control, and the giving is decidedly one-way— me to the audience.

I found that teaching private individual voice lessons to be more manageable for me than group class teaching as well. I knew I could handle more situations with a single person than the overwhelming stress of teaching a roomful of individuals. There were less variables that were prone to the unexpected, and I learned to mask very well during 1-1 interaction.

This was definitely a learned skill and not something that came naturally to me. But it came in handy when developing friendships and I was fortunately able to develop friendships as a child and into adulthood, and romantic/sexual relationships as I grew from childhood into adolescence and beyond. This is what gave me friends and lovers throughout my life.

This type of problem with large groups persisted when I substitute taught in later years. I tried to only accept assignments that were easy for me, which was normally the honors students who caused no trouble. But sometimes I ended up in situations where my autism was clear and on full display, though I did not know it at the time.

I remember one situation where I had a group of very young kids, they were Kindergarten or younger. There was something about an assembly and we were required to get them from point A to point B. For some reason I did not understand the directive or took it the wrong way and I was parading the kids through the hallways to get to the right spot. Somehow I got in big trouble over this and was taken off that school's substitute teaching list.

There was an incident with a high school student in a special ed class. I was supposed to watch this student constantly. But I went back into the classroom, or I let the student use the bathroom, something like that, and I got in trouble for letting the student be left unattended. So I was removed from that school's substitute list as well.

I remember an incident regarding a fellow teacher. Her son had just died and he was her only child. I was trying to be sympathetic but it did not go over very well. I began talking about my own son, what he was accomplishing, and how much I loved him, something like that. This must have upset the teacher a great deal because I was removed from the classroom for the rest of the day to go to a different classroom. I am not sure but I might have been removed from that assignment list as well.

It kind of came to a head when I was subbing in a high school where I ended up doing most of my subbing before leaving substitute teaching altogether. I was trying to use a school computer. Before the protocols were changed we were allowed to use the library computers without any login. I often used the library to check my email or other activities during my lunch break or free period. I ended up trying to use the computer that was in the faculty lounge. Apparently it was already logged into another teacher's account but I did not know this at all. As I was sitting there the teacher approached and basically said, "What do you think you're doing?" I explained that I was using the computer like I did in the library. This teacher became very irate with me and made a complaint to the principal and I was accused of being rude to her. I explained my rationale for my actions and also explained that at that time I was in the process of being evaluated for autism. I think it was that revelation to the principal that kept my position at that school when all the other positions were falling away from me. I taught there for several years before leaving substitute teaching altogether.

There was an incident at a partial hospitalization program which I attended after being hospitalized for cutting my wrist in a fit of frustration at my daughter. We were sitting in a circle. I truly hated those group therapy sessions, they never did anything for me. We were talking about something and a woman made some kind of inane comment. In response I said, "No shit, Sherlock!" Apparently the liver-bellied woman couldn't handle my directness and complained to the director, who *threw me out of a mental health treatment program*!!! I couldn't believe I did anything that inappropriate or disruptive to deserve that decision!!!

There was an incident when my grandson was born and he was admitted to the NICU for evaluation. My daughter was staying the Ronald McDonald house near the hospital and I was staying with her. I remember our staying in the NICU with my grandson overnight. I remember I had a big blanket they gave me and I remember walking around the hospital with the blanket draped around my shoulders. I am sure I looked rather deranged doing that.

At one point I was cuddled on a couch and someone came up to me and asked to look inside my blanket, as if I was hiding something in there. I must have been acting very strangely. Then something happened at the Ronald McDonald house and I was told I was forbidden from coming back there ever again.

There was an incident regarding a colleague of mine, a man who was my accompanist for the choir at the college where I taught. We had become close friends and we spent time eating together and talking a great deal. We had each other's phone numbers. At one point he did not want to accompany the choir anymore. I was not sure what I did but we did not have communication for several months. I knew he was also an organist at a certain church, so one day I decided to surprise him at the church.

He was very surprised indeed. We went out to lunch and were communicating again. Mind you, this man had mental illness and had tried to commit suicide and had a previous drug problem as well. But I remember calling him one day to see what he was up to. "Nothing," he said. "My boring life." I remember saying, "Well, if you want some company I could come hang out." Shortly after this I got a furious email from him telling me not to ever contact him again and that he did I would be reported for harassment. Not sure what I ever did to warrant that kind of ultimatum.

Another adult situation involved my years with the Mennonites. In my 30s I was in the wider circle of conservative Anabaptists, who practice a severe form of Christianity, a kind of religious fundamentalism. Women wear head coverings and modest, unadorned clothing. They practice a literal adherence to the words of the Bible. It's an autistic person's paradise—rigidity, inflexibility, habit, order, black and white thinking, literal interpretation of scripture. I was very happy during my years with them.

One of the issues is that my one-minded obsessive thinking could be interpreted as religious fervor. This is why I think many autistic people would be drawn into fundamentalism and even cults. I am sure this is the reason my autism remained hidden for so long, during the years when I was a fervent, devout, "on-fire," born-again evangelical, fundamentalist Christian.

The other issue that greatly affected my life is my tendency towards black-and-white thinking and literal interpretations of speech, directives, and words. For about ten years much of that kind of thinking was filtered through the conservative Anabaptist world I was in, but it also filtered through the homeschooling community, of which I was also part for many years. Largely because of this, I had a large family— larger than the average American family today. I took very literally the Biblical directive to "be fruitful and multiply" as well as the adage that a man is happy who has a "quiverfull" of children. We are also instructed to "let God plan your family" and that birth control was to be frowned upon. I truly believed that I would be going against God if I did not have as many children as I could "conceivably" have (pardon the pun). It was only after my 6th child did I endeavor not to have any more children. This is not to say that I am sorry in any way for my children. They are, along with my grandchildren, the greatest blessings of life to me. I am thankful and delighted with each of the thirteen souls that have sprung, directly or indirectly, from my loins. I am only pointing out the direct effects of literal thinking for an autistic person and how seeing the world in black-and-white can have very direct consequences in the outcome and course of an autistic person's life.

My supports coordinator remarked that it is highly unusual for an autistic woman to have children, let alone six children. But I have never fit the mold on most things.

I also literally believed in the interpretation I was taught about marriage. You are supposed to stay in a marriage, no matter what. If women do the right things then the men become the men they are supposed to be. This teaching influenced me to stay in my abusive marriage, and stay in it much longer than I should have. Black-and-white thinking, such as seen in autistic people, can indeed have dangerous and lasting consequences. My abusive marriage is discussed in great detail in my book *Warning Signs of Abuse: Get Out Early and Stay Free Forever.*

Lastly, I need to discuss cash registers. This also concerns counters like at the bank teller or customer service desk. I have always had a hard time at the cash register. First of all, when they ask you "Did you find everything you needed?" I find the question pointless and stupid. I usually respond, *"If I didn't, I certainly know how to ask for help!"* Dumb question! The other thing that truly bothers me to the core is the question "How are you?" First of all, that person does not care how I am. They could just say "Good morning" or "Hello." I find the question asked by complete strangers to be utterly intrusive and offensive. My favorite response to this question is, *"You don't give two shits in hell how I am, so why are you bothering to ask?"*

I have tried so many ways to avoid answering the question. Usually I start talking about how I want my things bagged, or something else, so as to avert the question. Saying something first usually diverts the conversation. If they manage to ask me, I try to ignore the question. Then the hard part comes because they might ask a second time. I have said, *"If I didn't answer you the first time, what makes you think I'm going to answer you the second time?"* Sometimes I will say something like, *"Nice weather today"* or something irrelevant to try to change the direction of the small talk. But I do find any small talk to be stupid, pointless, intrusive, and unnecessary.

Needless to say, this has caused a lot of embarrassment to people who are with me at the register, which usually involved my children, especially when they were younger. One of the solutions was to give the card to one of the kids and let them bag and pay. That actually relieved me of the stress of having to deal with the cash register situation at all.

There was an incident at the local post office. I went in there one day and I grew very irritated at the person at the counter because I thought she wasn't understanding me or she didn't have the intellectual capacity to understand my issue. Something happened and I remember have words with her and I remember slamming my butt on the door on my way out. I ended up getting a citation for disorderly conduct. I had to go to court to defend myself. Fortunately, the judge called her accusation "a tempest in a teapot" and dismissed the charge. But I still recognize my difficulties with counters and cash registers and service desks.

I think I got away with some of my behavior in public because I grew up in Manhattan and New Yorkers tend to be blunt and direct and a little abrasive. The rudeness that I am always accused of was glossed over because of my New York-ness.

I also think that my ability to adapt to new circumstances or new interests came from a primordial necessity to adapt during the first year of my life. Unlike most people I had three mothers by the time I was thirteen months old. That must have done something in me to cause me to be able to get deeply into something, and then move on to something else, and then to something else. It must have been a learned response from the earliest recesses of my psyche. I do get really into things to the point of near-obsession, but I can also start a new interest relatively easily and then get into that to the point of near-obsession. I am able to switch to new interests pretty easily. But one thing is for sure: I am always deeply interested in *something*, and I will learn about it, and study it, very thoroughly, until I become a near expert on it. And that one thing becomes my main focus for the duration of my learning or doing process. And I will want to tell you all about it. I will want to share all about it with you, in great detail, if you are willing to listen.

As you can see, I have had my fair share of social difficulties as an adult. My disability status is well-warranted and I am very grateful for the benefits it has provided me over the years. I have come to terms with my autism diagnosis. When I look back over the course of my life, I see the thread of autism weaving its way through every mishap, blunder, calamity, impropriety, slip-up, failure, and mishap in my social behavior. I was not depressed, or manic, but only my energetic, talkative self, getting into trouble over and over and over again. At least now I can make sense of it all, instead of my ignoring it or shoving it out of my memory or trying to forget that these things ever happened. I only want to go ahead from here with the help I have been provided with and try to be the best person I can be, as I go forward with the rest of my life.

CHAPTER FOUR: HOW I BECAME DISABLED

In my 20s I was diagnosed with bipolar disorder. I had gone to a hospital in New York City where the psychiatrist was very zealous about my diagnosis. I was put on a lithium regimen and had my blood drawn weekly.

I do remember telling them I felt "much better" being on the lithium. I did not know it at the time (and probably neither did the psychiatrist) but lithium has been used in autism treatment for symptoms such as irritability and agitation as well as mood symptoms. Looking back I definitely felt calmer and just better in general. It is no wonder that lithium was helpful to me as a person with autism.

But lithium made me gain weight and I got bad acne from it so I stopped using it. I was not on any psychiatric medications again until my 40s.

I started to have real problems after graduating with my master's degree in 2005 and began my teaching at the university as a lecturer. At this time I was also embroiled in an abusive marriage with a drug-using liar. We had tremendous financial problems and I was raising six kids basically as a single mother much of the time. Plus I had this very difficult position as a lecturer to groups of 25 to 40 kids at a time. It all piled up on top of me. I basically became non-functional and very unwell.

I ended up withdrawing from my teaching in the spring of 2008 due to "health reasons." At that point I was only conducting the campus choir anyway, so it was only one course. But I could hardly get out of bed.

I literally spent the better part of five years in bed. Yes, I did some things like grocery shop and take the kids here and there, but all my spare moments were spent in bed.

It was at this time, after I withdrew from the position, that I decided to apply for disability. I knew inside myself that I could never work a "real job" again and that virtually all my attempts in my entire life at working "real jobs" had failed miserably anyway.

Somewhere along the line I began seeing a psychiatrist. I had seen many over the years. I have been on a plethora of medications in various combinations and points over the years. My list included medications as Celexa, amitriptyline, Lexapro, Buspar, and Cymbalta for depression; mood stabilizers such as lithium, Lamictal, Topamax, and Depakote; anti-anxiety medications such as Ativan, hydroxyzine, pregabalin, Valium, and Xanax; and antipsychotics such as Abilify and Latuda.

I ended up gaining sixty pounds from my various combinations of psych medications over a span of several years. Many of them produced other disagreeable side effects. I used to call Topamax "Dope-amax" because of how stupid it made me feel. I used to get "Cymbalta jolts" in my brain when I came off of it or changed the dosage. The second time I tried lithium I could taste the metal on my tongue and got so nauseous I had to stop taking it.

Eventually I came out of the five-year state of non-functioning. I also was no longer depressed in any way. In fact I have not been depressed in over fourteen years. My behavioral supports specialist thinks what actually happened to me was an incident of PTSD (post-traumatic stress disorder). That makes a lot of sense to me and I am grateful for her insight and perspective. I am now trying to look at that period of my life through the lens of PTSD and it all becomes clearer when I do.

After my autism diagnosis, my psychiatric treatment basically shifted from treating bipolar disorder to treating my autism symptoms. I always struggled with agitation, angering easily, irritability, and hyper-reactivity to my environment. But now the emphasis was on allaying these symptoms rather than treating my moods.

Finally, after all these years, all the trials and errors, and all the various side effects, I am on a psychiatric regimen that is working for me. I take propranolol, which lowers my heart rate, and calms me, and Latuda, which really helps me with my irritability and reactivity to my environment. I also take melatonin and hydroxyzine as I go to bed and that helps my sleep in general.

When I initially applied for disability, I was rejected, which is the normal course for most people who apply. So I appealed.

I remember sitting in the hearing room with the judge. He went over my psychiatric history. I remember telling him, *"Do you really think I went back to school in my 40s to get a master's degree to end up like this?"* I remember him agreeing about that.

I finally received my disability status within about a half-year of my initial application, according to my memory. It may have been longer. But I have been on disability since 2008 and it has kept me alive all these years.

I just recently finally received the autism waiver after several years of waiting. This is helping me pay for the Medicaid portion of my insurance. It is also providing me with a supports coordinator who helps me get me into various services. I have recently begun to work with a behavioral supports specialist who is helping me with situations like my trouble at the cash registers. I look forward to learning some new solutions to my many and varied behavioral problems.

Me as a child, 1962- 1972.
That is my adoptive family, the Arlucks.

Me as a teenager, 1974-1979. The solo I was singing as a 17-year old earned me a standing ovation.

Me in my 20s, 1980-1988

My wedding day, 7/8/89, 27 years old

A year later as a new mother, 1990. My daughter Francesca

Angelica, born 1992

Anthony, born 1994

Gloria, born 1996

Gabriella, born 1998

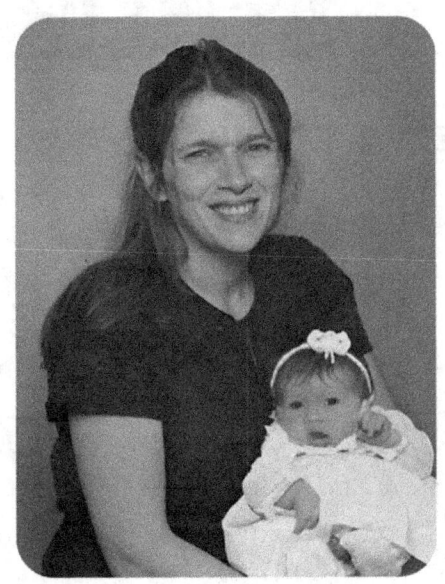

Sophia, born 2000

The family as children, 2000

2024

My professional headshot, when I was still singing and teaching, about 2004, age 42

Bachelor of Arts, vocal music performance, Skidmore College, 2001

Master of Music with distinction, voice pedagogy and performance, Westminster Choir College, 2005

At a poetry reading, about 2014

My default was singing
with my eyes closed

My mom and I at my final recital, 2015. I found her in 1984 and we've had a beautiful relationship all these years. The full story of our reunion is told in my book *When Adoption Fails: Abuse, Autism, and the Search for My Identity*

Leading from the center of the square at Sacred Harp, 2016

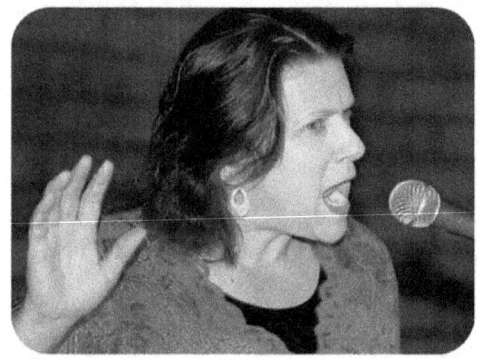

Promoting my book *Warning Signs of Abuse: Get Out Early and Stay Free Forever*, 2014

The intense singing of Sacred Harp

Still playing guitar after all these years

One of the greatest joys of my life:
reading my poetry publicly

My grandkids (left to right):
Julian, Theo, Jude, Aria, Max, Rosie, and Logan

All of us (plus my daughter-in-law) age 62, 2024

CHAPTER FIVE: MY AUTISM DIAGNOSIS

My son called me one day about nine years ago to talk to me about something that my daughter-in-law read in a Psychology 101 textbook in college. "Mom," he said, "Laura was reading some things about autism and she thinks that's what you have."

"*Bullshit*," I said. *"I am bipolar with anxiety. I don't have autism."*

"Well, you should look into it," he said.

My daughter-in-law actually said, "This sounds like your mom."

After a period of being utterly revulsed I decided to read a little and do a couple of those online quiz things. To my utter shock and surprise I really did score high on the autism tests. It was very unnerving to me. For years, I had interpreted all my mental health symptoms through the lens of bipolar disorder. I had been diagnosed with this in my 20s. My adoptive father had called me "manic" when I was young. But I realize now that I was just being my excited, talkative self. When I did get depressed I was just an autistic person who got depressed. I did not have mood swings as they presumed, because I had supposedly "mixed states" bipolar which means I was manic and depressed at the same time. If autism was not on the radar, it would not be beyond the realm of reasoned supposition to suspect my symptoms to be those of bipolar disorder.

I futzed around with this concept for quite some time before finally setting out to be evaluated for autism. The first center I went to told me that since I had a bipolar diagnosis, I would need to have those symptoms treated first, before they could evaluate me for autism. That was very frustrating and demoralizing.

My second attempt proved to be more fruitful.

I had a very enlightening interview with the psychologist who finally evaluated me. I rarely have felt understood by anyone like that in my entire life. I even asked her if she would be my counselor but she said she only did assessments and could not be my counselor. This left me dejected!

I am very fortunate that I have not only the reports from preschool in the 60s, and my report cards from grade school and junior high in the 60s and 70s, but I have the autism assessment from 2015. I think it presents a full picture of the person I am and always have been.

PENNSTATE HERSHEY
Medical Group
Psychological Assessment Report
CONFIDENTIAL

Name: Theresa Brown Werba
Date of Birth: 07/16/1962
Age: 53 years, 1 month

Medical Record #: [redacted] Date of Evaluation: 8/25/2015

Examiner: [redacted], Ph.D.

REFERRAL AND BACKGROUND INFORMATION
Reason for referral

Theresa Brown Werba referred herself for to rule-out a diagnosis of Autism Spectrum Disorder (ASD). Theresa reported chronic, significant difficulty with frustration tolerance, as well as social skills difficulties. Theresa currently indicated that she has a diagnosis of Bipolar Disorder and clinically significant anxiety.

EVALUATION COMPONENTS
Clinical Interview with Theresa Review of records
Social Responsiveness Scale, Second Edition (SRS 2; Self-Report)

Behavioral Observations: Theresa arrived at the office on time and readily accompanied the examiner to her office for the evaluation. Theresa was of average height and weight and was well dressed. She appeared anxious at the time of assessment. At times during the assessment she appeared to be extremely pressed to convey her thoughts and feelings with the examiner and was stressed about doing so. Her eye contact and affect was variable. Although her affect was appropriate to the situation, it was displayed in a higher intensity than expected indicating difficulty regulating and coping with negative affect. Theresa maintained normal speech and prosody. Her thought processes were normal and she was oriented to time and place. Overall, Theresa remained on-task for the majority of the time. There were times when the examiner redirected the topic of conversation as Theresa was anxious to provide an adequate amount of detail to facilitate the examiner's understanding of her experiences, thoughts, and feelings. Given her good effort, it is believed that the results of the assessment report represent a valid and reliable estimate of her true emotional and behavioral functioning.

DEVELOPMENTAL/SOCIAL/MEDICAL HISTORY

Theresa reported that she put up for adoption at the age of 3-months-old and was adopted at 13- months-old. No significant developmental concerns were noted. She reported that she did not have a good relationship with her adoptive father explaining that her adoptive father was emotionally abusive to her. Records (see multidisciplinary evaluation dated 4/21/2015) also indicate that Theresa reported a history of physical, sexual, and emotional abuse within her adoptive family. She indicated that she left her adoptive family's home at the of 15-years-old. Theresa reported that she has a history of chronic medical illnesses including fibromyalgia and Dercum's disease, as well as chronic back pain. Her records (see multidisciplinary evaluation dated 4/21/2015) also indicate that she has a history of gastroesophageal reflux disease, irritable bowel disease, Temporomandibular Joint (TMJ) Disorder, lactose intolerance, and petroleum sensitivities. It was also noted that she has been hospitalized in the past following a motor vehicle accident, a fractured lower extremity, ovarian cystectomy, pelvic floor reconstruction, shoulder separation repair, TMJ surgery, issues of recurrent candida infections, sleep apnea, and chronic insomnia.

Theresa reported that she was always very bright and did well academically in school. However, she did add that she had a history of behavior problems in the school setting. Theresa provided copies of several evaluations completed during preschool/elementary school years, as well as report cards and behavioral progress notes through elementary and middle school. The evaluations completed during her preschool years (see Developmental Report dated 2/15/1966 and 2/1967; Teacher Report dated 6/1966) noted that she displayed several areas of strength including a good vocabulary, good expressive language, has a natural musical ability and love for stories, has a good imagination within her art work, enjoyed working with manipulatives, and was sympathetic towards her peers. The report also mentioned that Theresa enjoyed talking to her teachers and having them listen to her. It was also noted that Theresa required significant accommodations to increase her focus and attention, as well as redirection to decrease impulsivity. It was also mentioned several times throughout reports from preschool and elementary school that Theresa "needed to develop self-control." Theresa was described as "an active child who has a drive to keep moving and very often does not look where she is going" and as a child who had a "desire to do many things at once." It was also stated that she had difficulty complying and following school routine, as well as with tolerating frustration and coping with negative affect (e.g., would cry when denied access to a toy another peer was using). A teacher report dated June, 1966 noted that Theresa "lack[ed] any awareness of breaking with group requirements," while a report to parents from school dated 1969/1970 noted that she has to develop the "need for allowing others to speak and to think of the rights of the group." It was also noted that she displayed significant difficulty taking turns during play with her peers and that "this... seemed most difficult for Theresa to understand." Finally, reports to parents from middle school mirrored concerns from elementary school, but were more vague in the reporting; specifically, it was noted that although conduct and behavior in the school environment was improving, Theresa still was exhibiting difficulty regulating her behavior in the classroom.

Theresa indicated that she has a Master's degree in music which was conferred in 2005. Theresa reported that she has a history of loving learning and feels that being in an academic setting, specifically in the creative arts, lends itself to tolerating individuals who have idiosyncrasies such as herself.

Theresa reported that she loves to write and has published four books and has written several articles for a magazine specializing in classical music. Theresa reported that she was previously a professor at Penn State, Berks and has since lost her job. She added that since that time she has taught as a substitute teacher in the past but found the experience overwhelming and stressful. Theresa stated that she had been in contact with the Office of Vocational Rehabilitation (OVR) in order to pursue services related to finding appropriate work that she is able to engage in. Theresa stated that she is currently receiving disability and teaches individual voice lessons approximately three hours per week at a school in Reading, Pennsylvania.

Theresa reported that her social difficulties have become more significant and impairing as she has aged. She explained that she becomes significantly stressed during social conversations. For example, she reported that she does not know where to insert herself into a conversation and where conversations are "supposed" to stop and start. Theresa reported that she find auditory stimuli "intense" and difficult to tolerate at times. She added that she has been informed by others that she speaks in a loud tone, but noted that she does not perceive it this way. She explained that this is perplexing to her as she finds some noises overwhelming herself. Theresa reported that she will "get fixated on things" or topics that her children will comment are unexpected. She stated that they have said that she becomes interested in things "to the point of obsessiveness." Theresa reported that several areas of interest for her include canals, as well as Shakespeare and Shakespearean writing. She explained that she will "talk about [these topics] with fervor." In regards to relationships, Theresa reported that she currently is divorced and that this was finalized in 2010. She reported that prior to this she was married for 21 years. She indicated that she has six children from her marriage, one of which still resides in the home with her. She also added that she has three grandchildren. Theresa reported that approximately a year prior to the initial intake session that her son, who is in college, suggested that she may have Asperger's Disorder.

    Theresa stated that she experiences significant discrepancies in skill ability in several areas of her life. For example, she described herself as excelling in certain areas of musicianship, but struggling in others (e.g., sight-reading music). She also stated that although she is likes to write and is a published author, she has significant difficulty typing on a keyboard. Therefore, she noted that this makes the task of writing exceedingly difficult to accomplish and frustrating as she feels that these areas of strengths and difficulties are discrepant.

    Theresa reported that she experiences significant anxiety while around crowds. Additionally, she reported that she has a difficult time tolerating mistakes. For example, she stated that if she becomes aware that a mistake is made in something that she has written (e.g., a comma where it should be a semicolon), she will have significant difficulty leaving it as a comma. Theresa stated that she "cannot tolerate stupidity" in other people. For example, she indicated that while checking out at a grocery store the cashier asked her if she found everything ok; she explained that her immediate thought was "of course I did, or I would not be checking out." Theresa also reported that she finds it incredibly frustrating when people engage in social niceties, for example when people ask "How are you?" in a public, retail setting. She explained that she is annoyed with this as she does not believe that they are genuinely interested in her well-being. Theresa reported significant difficulty tolerating frustration. She indicated that when she was in her late 20's that she pushed the cash register on the floor at a take-out food restaurant when the individual informed her that they were out of the food that she had ordered. She reported that she is distraught over this behavior and does not understand why she had this reaction. Theresa reported that in the past she has "made poor decisions" which suggests significant clinical impulsivity and/or symptoms of mania. She stated that one example was "marrying her husband" who she reported was abusive within the relationship prior to the marriage.

Theresa reported that she has a history of diagnoses of Bipolar I Disorder with Mixed States and anxiety. She reported that she has seen several psychiatrists over the years, but has had significant side effects to several medications prescribed to stabilize her mood. She reported that her primary care physician is currently prescribing her Abilify (5mg) which she started the week prior to the initial intake session. She reported that she is tolerating it well so far and feels as if it is reducing her mood lability. Theresa reported that she has been hospitalized in a psychiatric hospital twice in the past. She also added that she has participated in a partial hospitalization program. She reported that she had significant difficulties participating in group therapy during her partial hospitalization and stated that she was "thrown out" of the group for making a comment to another group member that was interpreted as rude and disrespectful.

Theresa's records also indicate that she was assessed for ASD at the Center for Autism and Developmental Disabilities (CADD) at Philhaven in April, 2015 (see multidisciplinary evaluation dated 4/21/2015). These results indicate that her ADOS 2 score fell in the range indicating a likely diagnosis of ASD (ADOS 2 Total Score = 15), but that this was rule-out and the symptoms were noted as being better accounted for by her diagnoses of Bipolar Disorder and Generalized Anxiety Disorder. Theresa reported that she is looking for an outpatient therapist to help her work on social skills, as well as a psychiatrist to manage her medications for

Bipolar Disorder and anxiety symptoms. Theresa reported that she has developed several methods of coping over the years including keeping a routine and schedule which helps reduce negative affect and stabilize her mood.

Autism Spectrum Disorder Assessment

The following is a summary of the symptoms of Autism Spectrum Disorder obtained through an unstructured interview, as well as the Social Responsiveness Scale, Second Edition completed by Theresa. To meet criteria for Autism Spectrum Disorder, all items in Section A and a total of two (or more) items from Section B need to be endorsed. To meet criteria for Social (Pragmatic) Communication Disorder there needs to be evidence of persistent difficulties in the social use of verbal and nonverbal communication, but the criteria for Autism Spectrum Disorder is not met (no restricted, repetitive patterns of behavior, interests, or activities are present).

A. Persistent deficits in social communication and social interaction across multiple contexts, as manifested by the following, currently or by history:

1. Deficits in social-emotional reciprocity (e.g., abnormal social approach, failure of back- and-forth conversation, reduced sharing of interests/emotions/affect, failure to initiate or respond to social interactions). Theresa reported a history of difficulty with reciprocal conversations. Theresa explained that she becomes significantly stressed during social

conversations. For example, she reported that she does not know where to insert herself into a conversation and where conversations are "supposed" to stop and start. On the SRS 2, Theresa reported that she is awkward in turn-taking interactions with others (for example, she has a hard time keeping up with the give-and-take of a conversation). She also noted that almost always her behavior is socially awkward, even when she is trying to be polite. Theresa also reported on the SRS 2 that she does not enjoy small talk (casual conversations with others) and that often her way of greeting another person is unusual.

2. Deficits in nonverbal communicative behaviors used for social interaction (e.g., poorly integrated verbal and nonverbal communication, abnormalities in eye contact and body language/gestures, lack of facial expressions and nonverbal communication). During the unstructured interview, Theresa displayed spontaneous descriptive gestures, as well as some emphatic or emotional gestures. However, these gestures were not in sync with or used to regulate the social interaction with the examiner. On the SRS 2, Theresa reported that she often avoids eye contact or has been told that she has unusual eye contact and almost always gets overly loud without realizing it. Theresa also reported that almost always her facial expressions send the wrong message to others about how she actually feels. She also added that almost always others feel that she has an overly serious facial expression. Additionally,

she reported that when people change their tone or facial expression, she usually does not pick up on that and understand what it means. Finally, she added that she sometimes gets too close to others or invades their personal space without realizing it and often makes the mistake of walking between two people who are trying to talk to one another.

3. Deficits in developing, maintaining, and understanding relationships (e.g., difficulties adjusting behavior to suit various social contexts, difficulties in sharing imaginative play or in making friends, absence of interest in peers). On the SRS 2, Theresa reported that she sometimes has difficulty making friends, even when she is trying her best. As previously noted Theresa stated that she does not understand the use of social niceties in casual social interactions, such as a cashier asking her if she found everything ok and when people ask "how are you?" in a public, retail setting. She explained that she is annoyed with the latter example as she does not believe that they are genuinely interested in her well-being. Theresa explained that people inform her that she is frequently rude to them, but she does not understand why others perceive her this way. During the unstructured interview, Theresa showed some insight into several social relationships, but historically reported having difficulty articulating her own role within it although she has voiced having become more cognizant of this as she has aged.

B. Restricted, repetitive patterns of behavior, interests, or activities:

1. Stereotyped or repetitive motor movements, use of objects, or speech (e.g., simple motor stereotypies, lining up toys, flipping objects, echolalia, idiosyncratic phrases). During the unstructured interview, Theresa was not observed to display stereotyped or repetitive motor movements.

2. Insistence on sameness, inflexible adherence to routines, or ritualized patterns of verbal or nonverbal behavior (e.g., distress at small changes, difficulties with transition, rigid thinking patterns, greeting rituals, need to take same route or eat same food every day). On the SRS 2, Theresa reported that she often has more difficulty than others with changes in her routine and is often inflexible. Theresa reported being upset by change and significant difficulty tolerating frustration. As noted previously, she indicated that when she was in her late 20's that she pushed a cash register on the floor at a take-out food restaurant when he/she informed her that they were out of the food that she had ordered. She also reported a significant history of rigid thinking patterns. Again, as noted previously Theresa stated that she has a difficult time tolerating mistakes. Finally, Theresa's school records indicated that she was often reluctant to stop one activity and begin another.

3. Highly restricted, fixated interests that are abnormal in intensity or focus (e.g., strong attachment to or

preoccupation with unusual objects, excessively circumscribed or she is interested in too few topics or that she gets too carried away with these topics. perseverative interests). On the SRS 2, Theresa reported that almost always people think Theresa reported that she will "get fixated on things" or topics that her children will comment are unexpected. She stated that they have said that she becomes interested in things "to the point of obsessiveness." Theresa reported that several areas of interest for her include canals, as well as Shakespeare and Shakespearean writing. She explained that she will "talk about [these topics] with fervor."

4. Hyper- or hyporeactivity to sensory input or unusual interest in sensory aspects of the environment (e.g., apparent indifference to pain/temperature, adverse response to specific sounds or textures, excessive smelling or touching of objects, visual fascination with lights or movement). On the SRS 2, Theresa reported that she is almost always overly sensitive to certain sounds, textures, or smells. Theresa reported that she find auditory stimuli "intense" and difficult to tolerate at times. She added that she has been informed by others that she speaks in a loud tone, but noted that she does not perceive it this way. She explained that this is perplexing to her as she finds some noises overwhelming herself.

Theresa displays a number of characteristics that are consistent with a diagnosis of Autism Spectrum Disorder (A1, A2, A3, B2, B4); therefore, she does meet criteria for a diagnosis of ASD. It should be noted that although there are significant symptoms reported in the area of B3, it is unclear as to whether these related to symptoms of Bipolar Disorder or ASD. Additionally, Theresa's own ratings of her behavior on the SRS 2 fell in the severe range (SRS 2 Total T-score =78).

Social Responsiveness Scale (SRS 2)

Scale Score	T Score	Classification
Social Awareness	72	Moderate
Social Cognition	79	Severe
Social Communication	75	Moderate
Social Motivation	76	Severe
Restricted and Repetitive Behaviors	74	Moderate
Social Communication Impairment	78	Severe

Restricted and Repetitive Behaviors
74
Moderate
SRS Total Score
78
Severe

Ratings of Theresa's own behavior were highest on scales which assess an individual's the ability to interpret social cues once they are picked up, cognitive-interpretive aspects of reciprocal social behavior (social cognition), as well as on a scale which measures the extent to which a respondent is generally motivated to engage in social-interpersonal behavior (social motivation). Theresa rated her behavior in the moderate range on scales which measured her ability to pick up on social cues, sensory aspects of social behavior (social awareness), her communication) and one which measures the stereotypical behaviors or highly restricted expressive social communication, "motoric" aspects of reciprocal social behavior (social interests characteristic of autism (restricted and repetitive behaviors).

SUMMARY

Theresa Brown Werba referred herself for to rule-out a diagnosis of Autism Spectrum Disorder (ASD). Theresa reported significant difficulty with frustration tolerance, as well as social skills difficulties. Theresa currently indicated that she has a diagnosis of Bipolar Disorder and clinically significant anxiety. A review of the information obtained from the clinical interview and the SRS 2 indicates that Theresa is reporting moderate impairment in the areas of social awareness, social communication, and restricted and repetitive behaviors. She is reporting severe impairment in social cognition and social motivation, as well as in the overall area of social communication. Her overall score on the SRS 2 falls in the severe range. Theresa displays persistent deficits in social communication and social interaction across multiple contexts, as manifested by deficits in social-emotional reciprocity, deficits in nonverbal communicative behavior, and deficits in developing, maintaining, and understanding relationships. Additionally, Theresa displays restricted, repetitive patterns of behavior, interests, or activities as manifested by insistence on sameness, inflexible adherence to routines, or ritualized patterns of verbal or nonverbal behavior, highly restricted, fixated interests that are abnormal in intensity or focus, and hyperreactivity to sensory input or unusual interests in sensory aspects of the environment. The symptoms are reported to be not better accounted for by her comorbid diagnoses of Bipolar Disorder and anxiety, they are chronic, and cause clinically significant impairment in social and occupational functioning.

DIAGNOSTIC IMPRESSIONS
299.0 Autism Spectrum Disorder

Criteria A: Requiring support (Level 1)
Criteria B: Requiring support (Level 1)
Without accompanying intellectual impairment Without accompanying language impairment
296.40 Bipolar Disorder, Type I, Unspecified (Mixed States by history) Unspecified Anxiety Disorder (by history)
300.0
RECOMMENDATIONS

Theresa is experiencing significant mental health impairment in multiple areas including anxiety in addition to her current diagnosis of Bipolar Disorder. Additionally, she meets criteria for Autism Spectrum Disorder (ASD). Given that Theresa has several areas of significant concern, will be extremely important for her to work with mental health and medical professionals that are coordinating her care. It is recommended that the following be addressed in the order presented below to maximize Theresa's functioning:

1. Services for Adults with ASD. Given a diagnosis of ASD, Theresa will qualify for state- funded services. The Pennsylvania Department of Public Welfare's Bureau of Autism Services (BAS) provides services to adults with ASD, including the Adult Autism Waiver. As of now, this is the only program available in Theresa's county of residence. The goals of these programs are to increase self-care and independence, decrease family stress, provide supports for employment and community involvement and decrease crises and

hospitalization. At this time, these programs are not taking new clients. However, Theresa should be placed on the waiting list for services when the do so, the Bureau of Autism Services should be contacted at 1.866.539.7689 or email RA-odpautismwaiver@pa.gov for the Adult Autism Waiver. The ASERT Statewide Resource Center (see below for contact information) can be of assistance in accessing

>these services.

>program re-opens.

>2. Services for Adults with Mental Health Diagnoses. Given a diagnosis of Bipolar Disorder and Unspecified Anxiety Disorder, Theresa will qualify for community-based services through county-based mental health services, including the Office of Vocational Rehabilitation. Services that are often easier to access are specific for general mental health issues and are not specific for ASD. It is still recommended that while Theresa is on wait lists for ASD specific services that she access what services she can to help support her ability to maximize her functioning. The ASERT Statewide Resource Center (see below for contact information) can also be of assistance in accessing these services. 3. Support Groups for Adults with ASD. Theresa may find emotional support, as well as information about accessing services and help by exploring support groups for individuals with ASD. The majority of these groups target children and adolescents with ASD and their families; however, some groups focus solely on supporting adults with ASD. Information about support groups can be

found at www.paautism.org (autism Community → Support Groups) or by calling the Statewide ASERT Resource Center (see below for contact information).

    4. Medication Consultation. Theresa will likely benefit from medication for symptoms of Bipolar Disorder and/or anxiety. It should be noted that there are no medications that directly treat symptoms of ASD. Providers who manage medications for individuals with ASD are treating symptoms of comorbid psychopathology such as anxiety, depression, or irritability. Given Theresa's current diagnoses, it is recommended that Theresa seek an evaluation for medication by a psychiatrist or nurse practitioner with expertise in Bipolar Disorder. If Theresa is interested in a referral to the Mood Disorders Clinic at Penn State Hershey, she should contact the adult clinic coordinator at xxx-xxxx to schedule an appointment. Given that this program is housed within Penn State Hershey, this will allow providers within the Mood Disorders Clinic to consult with providers in the Autism Division who would be available to consult and assist as needed with Theresa's care. It should be noted that Penn State Hershey Psychiatry's mission in addition to clinical care is training and research. Therefore, the majority of physicians at Penn State Hershey Psychiatry are residents whose practice is overseen by an attending physician, so it is likely that Theresa would be seen by a resident physician in training. Additionally, the Mood Disorders Clinic is also collecting data on each patient upon their consent for research purposes to better

understand how to improve treatment for individuals with Mood Disorders. Therefore, patients being treated, if they consent, will be asked to complete a significant amount of questionnaires for data collection as part of their care To facilitate being seen, Theresa should send a copy of her entire medical records to our clinic to do so). For other referrals for providers in the area, Theresa should contact her healthcare insurance company for a list of providers that accept her insurance. When contacting these providers, she should look for individuals who have expertise in treating adults with Bipolar Disorder.

    5. Psychological Interventions for Comorbid Mood and Anxiety Symptoms. Theresa is experiencing significant internalizing symptoms both related to depression associated with her Bipolar Disorder diagnosis, as well as additional anxiety. These symptoms are currently moderate to severe and have likely been impacting Theresa's life for years. Following a stabilization of symptoms through medication, it is recommended that residual symptoms be addressed in individual therapy using an empirically supported therapy with a cognitive-behavioral framework with a therapist who has experience working with individuals with Bipolar Disorder. Therefore, I will defer to the Mood Disorders Clinic, or other experts in this area, in regards to recommendations for therapy for symptoms of Bipolar Disorder. Given Theresa's diagnosis of ASD, the general treatment goals and methods used in therapy for these symptoms will hold; however, these

providers and Theresa should be aware that the prognosis and methods used may need to be adapted given Theresa's ASD diagnosis. One local option for individual therapy would be Riverside Associates, P.C. in Harrisburg, PA (717.238.6880) as they specialize in treating adults with ASD.

    6. Social Skills Groups for Adults with ASD. Theresa is currently experiencing significant difficulties with social skills related to her diagnosis of ASD. The best treatment for these symptoms include a combination of varied methods of instruction such as discussion- based skills building, video modeling for social skills, and generalization experiences with typically developing peer models in a group setting. As with the support groups individuals with ASD, the majority of social skills groups target children, adolescents, and young adults. Therefore, it may be somewhat difficult to find a social skills group for adults over the age of 30-years-old. Additionally, Theresa has reported a history of significant difficulties working in a group setting. Therefore, enrolling in a social skills group should be considered following stabilization of symptoms associated with Theresa's diagnosis of Bipolar Disorder and frustration intolerance. The best resource for this information regarding available social skills groups for adults will also be the Statewide ASERT Resource Center (see below for contact information). Again, one local option for adult social skills groups would be Riverside Associates, P.C. in Harrisburg, PA (717.238.6880) as they specialize in treating adults with ASD.

7. Additional sources for information. Several additional web-based resources are available to individuals with ASD and emotional difficulties. Theresa may wish to access the following:

Theresa is encouraged to call the ASERT Autism Resource Center, 1 (877) 231- 4244 or visit www.paautism.org for additional information regarding the recommendations noted above, as well as for any future questions or concerns regarding services and/or treatment.

b. Theresa may benefit from visiting websites for individuals with ASD, such as www.autismspeaks.org and www.autism-society.org.

c. National Institute for Mental Health (http://www.nimh.nih.gov) is the largest scientific organization in the world dedicated to research focused on understanding, treatment, and prevention of mental disorders and the promotion of mental health. d. National Alliance on Mental Illness (http://www.nami.org) offers information on educational programs and support groups for individuals with mental illnesses.

e. Anxiety and Depression Association of America (http://www.adaa.org) offers information on anxiety and depression, including facts about internalizing symptoms, self-help resources, and a searchable database for finding a therapist.

Thank you for the opportunity to work with you. I hope that the results of this assessment will be helpful in improving your current functioning.

[redacted], Ph.D.
Assistant Professor
Licensed Psychologist

Needless to say, this detailed and comprehensive report was like gold to me. I finally had the answers as to the mysteries and perplexities of my entire life. I welled with tears and I was glad and sad at the same time— glad because it was making sense now, and sad because I had so many things happen to me because of my autism that I could not control or understand at the time. I was very grateful that I was finally understood, and I was truly vindicated.

Thus after a lifetime of issues, questions, perplexities, problems, enigmas, conundrums, and wonderings, I was evaluated for autism and diagnosed in 2015 at the age of 53.

CHAPTER SIX: SINCE MY DIAGNOSIS

In the nine years since my diagnosis life has gone from good to better to best. How peaceful and restorative life has been! In some ways my later years have been my very best years, and my 60s the best decade of my life so far.

My ex-husband died in 2017 and that relieved me of a great deal of stress. My relationship with him is covered in my book *Warning Signs of Abuse: Get Out Early and Stay Free Forever*. Like I said in the book, my life has been better now that he is no longer in it. The amount of stress and anguish that that relationship inflicted upon me contributed significantly, if not primarily, to the decline in my mental health and my overall functioning when I was so unwell in the 2010s. Although the children miss him and it has been hard for them, I have never been more happy and content and at peace since he's been gone.

I also discovered my biological father since I was diagnosed, and found out that his brother, my biological uncle, also has autism. He has lived alone his whole adult life. I wrote to him but he never responded. I hope he is happy and getting the assistance he needs to function in life. The story of my adoption, and the discovery of my Jewish father, is covered in my book *When Adoption Fails: Abuse, Autism, and the Search for My Identity*.

In the last few years I studied Hebrew for fourteen months as well as took a course in Basic Judaism as well as a survey of Talmud at my local synagogue. I also sing with the choir and have been attending shabbat and other services. I am preparing myself for the commitment to joining the Jewish people and formally converting to Judaism at a future date. When I found out my biological father was Jewish, it all made sense to me why I was always drawn to the Jewish people and feel my home among them.

My six children are all grown and doing extremely well. Their occupations are graphic designer/artist/creative director and mother of two, social worker and mother of three, software engineer and father of two, attorney, tech start-up entrepreneur, and biologist/soon-to-be medical student. In spite of the stress of growing up in a home where their father was a drug addict who abused their autistic mother, they have turned out extremely well. I am so thankful that they are high functioning and are free from any serious mental illness. However, there is high symptomatology of ADHD symptoms in 4 out of 6 of them. Each of those children are trying to get treatment for it at this time. It is known that autism and ADHD are linked and that various types of neurodivergence runs in families, expressing itself differently among the various members.

My grandchildren, all seven of them, are remarkably funny and smart and creative and beautiful. Three of them have been diagnosed with ADHD and one of those we do suspect is on the autism spectrum. He is going to be re-evaluated and we are hoping this will help him in his education and course of life.

I have been able to obtain my own housing because of my disability status and I am happily living in my own apartment. I have lots to keep me busy. I help my daughter-in-law once a week with laundry and my daughter once a week with laundry and babysitting. I am also called upon to babysit at various times and I am glad my life is flexible enough at this time to be available to help out.

I also am an accomplished seamstress and I do things like make dolly dresses and mend things and make quilts and make clothes. I am glad I learned this skill as a child and I have used it throughout my life.

Unfortunately I have not been playing the piano as I used to do. I got frustrated with the current state of ability and skill level and just gave up. I know I need to get back to it so I hope I can get myself back in the groove before too long.

I don't sing professionally as a soloist anymore, nor am I teaching voice anymore, though I do sing with the synagogue choir from time to time because they need sopranos. For about ten years I sang Sacred Harp with the local group in my area. Sacred Harp is a form of American folk music of a sacred nature that involves singing 4-part choral music without accompaniment. It is rigorous and raw and powerful. It involves singing primarily from a book called *The Sacred Harp* and the music does not derivate. It involves customs and rituals of practice and socialization, which provide a sense of constancy and regularity. Within the Sacred Harp community is a range of religious, political, gender-expression, neurodivergence, and age groups. You would have an Old Order River Brethren woman or Mennonite in a cape dress and head covering sitting next to a tattooed punk rocker with body piercings. It is a place where being different is okay, and even expected, and you can really be yourself there. The repetitive nature and constancy of the whole experience was very comforting to me and I loved my time being part of the Sacred Harp community.

I read at poetry events and readings from time to time, and employ my ability to perform in front of an audience to great effect. Nobody is ever bored when they listen to me read! It has been said of me that my recitations have "all the passions of high theater." I am grateful that I have been able to segue my performing abilities from singing to poetry recitations. I am never happier than when I am reading my poetry in front of an audience.

I have been studying a lot, as is my usual custom. I listen to audio books and lectures and read on a great deal on various topics. My current interests have been the fall of the Roman Empire/Late Antiquity, Jewish history and religion (including Mussar, Kabbalah, and Talmud), the development of the New Testament canon and the rise of Christianity, historical linguistics, and famous true crime cases. I also listen to classic novels while I am swimming. They have been novels which I never read previously but are novels I "should" have read. I recently finished Jane Austin's *Sense and Sensibility*, George

Elliot's *Daniel Deronda,* Harriet Beecher Stowe's *Uncle Tom's Cabin,* Elliot's *Middlemarch,* and have recently finished Charles Dickens' *Bleak House.*

I also have finally gotten into a beautiful routine which gives me great peace and joy. I didn't always have a real routine because my earlier life was very chaotic; I think that not having a routine contributed to my mental imbalance and stress and depression in the years that I was so unwell. But now that I have the opportunity for routine, I am happier and feel better and am less stressed and anxious.

But every morning I start with my simple prayers. After weighing myself (I had weight loss surgery over a year ago) I make my coffee. I like my coffee the same way every day. Then I do my morning puzzles. I do several from the New York Times: Strands (where you find words in a kind of word search), Wordle (where you guess a 5-letter word through process of elimination), Connections (where you find words that share a common thread or theme), Spelling Bee (a kind of text twist), the Mini crossword, and Letterboxed (where you form words around a square of letters). I also play five Scrabble games at any one time. They are fun and also very calming to my spirit and doing them makes me happy. They set me up for a good day. Then I also write my mother a morning email and we usually also write a p.m. email as well. I don't like to deviate from this routine as it is working very well for me and gives me happiness and joy in life.

I have spent a great deal of time on my writing, particularly my poetry. I now have published four books of poetry and five other books. My first collection is *Jesus and Eros: Sonnets, Poems, and Songs*, which juxtaposes spiritual issues with various types of poetry involving love. The songs in the book are songs I actually wrote and sang during my time as a singer. My second collection is *Longer Thoughts*, which compiles some of my longer poetry that accumulated since *Jesus and Eros*. My third poetry books is *Sonnets*, a collection of sixty-five sonnets in Shakespearean, Spenserian, and Petrarchan forms. My fourth collection is what I think is my magnum opus: *What Was and Is: Formal Poetry and Free Verse*. It is truly a beautiful and powerful collection of my best work over the last forty years.

I have written a book entitled *Warning Signs of Abuse: Get Out Early and Stay Free Forever*. It seeks to help women get out of early relationships that have shown signs of becoming abusive. My book *When Adoption Fails: Abuse, Autism, and the Search for My Identity* tells the story of my conception, adoption, growing up in an abusive home, and finding my both my biological parents. I wrote *Diaper Changes: The Complete Diapering Book and Resource Guide* over thirty years ago, when I was a mother of young children.

And of course you are reading *Finally Autistic: Finding My Autism Diagnosis as a Middle-Aged Female*. I hope you are enjoying learning about my life as an autistic female. Perhaps you will read another one of my books. I truly hope so.

The only problem with my writing is my handwriting and typing ability. I am a terrible typist. I literally have mistakes with every single sentence that I type, sometimes nearly every word. Sometimes it involves inverting letters and sometimes it is just typing the wrong letter or groups of letters. It is incredibly frustrating to me. The same goes for my handwriting. I usually switch letters and I often leave out letters from words when I write. It is very vexing and unnerving to me. It takes me twice as long as it should to type things because of the amount of corrections I have to do all along the process. I must have a mild form of dyslexia, and it can co-exist in a person with autism.

I am not in any relationship nor do I have any desire to be. Most of my adolescent and adult life involved myriad loves and losses, and I am happy now in being single, unencumbered, without attachment, and alone.

I love being alone. I am never lonely when I am alone. I love the peace and tranquility it brings me. I love the lack of stress of it. I love the happiness it brings me. I love the perfection of it. I am filled with joy and delight when I can be by myself. There, within my mind, is the fullness of all my interests and projects and creativity and discoveries. Now that my children are grown and I am living alone for the first time since my 20s, I am so delighted with being able to come home every day to peace and quiet and solitude. I love solitude. It is never a lonely place but a place of exciting potential and a well of knowledge and learning. It is a place where I can truly be myself without having to explain or apologize. My autism means nothing in the context of web searches, books read, books and poetry written, lectures and podcasts listened to, sewing projects undertaken, even cooking executed for just one person. I love being able to go where I want to, when I want to, and answer to no one. I love the autonomy of solitude. This is where I can truly be who I am, and always have been. Solitude is not loneliness, it is contentment!

I have the full and happy relationships with my six children, and the delight of my seven grandchildren. With them I can be myself with no masking and they know who I am and they tolerate me as I am to the best of their ability. I try not to be irritating but I know I have gotten on their nerves at times and embarrassed them many times. So I try to be the best I can be with my children. I have only a couple of true "friends" but I surely mask with them and I do my best to make the relationship abound in verbal reciprocity.

I have started working with an excellent behavioral supports specialist through the autism waiver, who is working with me on my social situations and frustration tolerance and how to manage both of these situations better. She is literally a godsend to me. It took nine years to get to her and now I wonder how I ever got along without her. Her insight, suggestions, and understanding have become invaluable to me. I look forward to improving how I interact with people at the most superficial levels as well as better managing my poor frustration tolerance.

I accept my autism diagnosis now and it is part of me. I try not to make it my identity but because of my ongoing issues and problems it is always rearing its head at me. I try to be tolerant and forgiving of myself when I fail in social situations. I am trying to accept my diagnosis as the explanation for much of my life, perhaps most of my life. I am very, very thankful that this was finally brought to the light, and I am glad that there is an explanation for what was once the unexplainable past. My present and future are bright and optimistic and I look forward to many more years as a writer, poet, mother and grandmother.

CHAPTER SEVEN: ASPERGER'S SPEAKS

Asperger's Speaks
Asperger Syndrome, first identified in 1944, was reclassified as Autism Level 1, part of Autism Spectrum Disorder, in the DSM-5 of 2013.

In a world of hyper-stimuli,
Lights and sounds and touches,
I retreat into the world within myself
for relief.

There is too much to process
all at once,
It comes at me like a screaming hoard,
shoving up against my walls
and forcing me to interact.

Why interact? Most talk like that is
stupid, pointless, irrational.
*If you do not care how I am today,
why do you ask me how I am? Just say
Good Morning or Hello!*

It is this stupid, slow world,
Where I move faster, think better,
process factually,
that frustrates me.

*And when you talk, do I
really understand? Why is it
that we misalign, why do
I misperceive what you are saying?
Is this why you are frustrated
with me?*

*Why is my voice too loud,
my speech too intense?
Why do you think I'm being rude,
when I am just annoyed?*

You do not like the things I like,
the things that interest me,
and I could talk unimpeded
for hours about these
very interesting things
unless you stopped me.

It could be canals, or the Shakespearean authorship issue,
or points of linguistics,

or the study of late Antiquity, or Jewish history,
or poetry— my poetry.

You do not understand the tiny things
that matter so much to me, or why they do,
why I must tell you every detail,
every minutiae, why I have to explain,
must explain
everything, every little thing.

My mental world is overloaded and then
I go outside where the world
is overloaded and then
I can do no more.

At times it seems I do not even care
because in that moment it is simply
not available for me to care.

But inside myself, my heart
is wide, and deep,
so deep I have to shut it off
in order to get through the
interactions into which
I must engage.

*Why has it been so hard
to walk into a store,
or interact in public?*

*Must I always play the game,
must I always act, pretend,
and be somebody else
just to buy something?*

My mind explodes
with ideas, thoughts,
learning and logic,
connections and observations,
but when to stop, and when to give you
a turn to speak
evades me.

I am learning to do this to this very day.

Without the social mask, I'm sure
you would not like me;
being myself is one long conversation
with myself.

But I have learned to smile,
to look into your eyes,
to be politic when necessary

(though I hate necessity),
to play the nice game of
interaction.

If you would only understand!
My heart is not my
talking, but I am truly
trying to reach you through my
talking, and so I'm talking,
on and on and on and on and on.

For rages come, and anger,
the cursing, the frustrations,
the rantings.
Why is everyone so stupid?
Why am I in a world of idiots?
Why doesn't this person
have a brain?

Perhaps my only disability
is my intelligence.
My hyper-wired brain
is both an advantage
and a defect.

Rigid and inflexible to sudden change,
it sends me into spasms

as I try to figure out what
is now going on.
But it is not supposed to be this way!
That's not what the menu said!
That's not what you told me before!

What I cannot process I therefore cannot understand,
And the world then makes me angry
and frustrated.

Only in the confines and restrictions
of my bed, my routine morning puzzles,
my daily evening internet,
am I at equilibrium.

Here it is I can find the quiet
absent within my own mind.

So when I talk, that is truly me,
trying to get out, one iota of the cosmos
within, one speck of the vast
universe of my thoughts.

Wouldn't you like to join this world and
listen for a little while?

So, be patient with me, try to listen through,
try to understand,
because inside I am very, very alone,
just my thoughts and me,
trying to be heard.

AFTERWORD

I am delighted that you have read *Finally Autistic*. Thank you for allowing me to share a portion of my complicated life story with you. I am very grateful for your listening ear and receptive heart.

I hope you will consider reading more of my work: my four poetry books are *Jesus and Eros: Sonnets, Poems and Songs*, which is a collection of poetry arranged into three distinct categories; *Longer Thoughts* a collection of longer poems; *Sonnets*, a collection of sixty-five sonnets in Shakespearean, Spenserian, and Petrarchan forms a *What Was and Is: Formal Poetry and Free Verse* which explores the creative process, love and loss, aging, notable historical figures, neurodivergence, and religious disillusionment in free verse as well as forms such as the sonnet, villanelle, ode, pantoum, and triolet, as well as nonce forms.

In *When Adoption Fails: Abuse, Autism, and the Search for My Identity* you will discover even more about my life as an undiagnosed autistic adoptee, who endured an abusive home and found both my birth mother and father. In *Warning Signs of Abuse* I give help for women in the beginning stages of an abusive relationship.

Find me on social media @thesonnetqueen and my website at www.theresawerba.com.
Theresa Werba 2024

www.ingramcontent.com/pod-product-compliance
Lightning Source LLC
Chambersburg PA
CBHW072054290426
44110CB00014B/1679